Artists Through the Ages

Paul Gauguin

Alix Wood

WINDMILL
BOOKS

New York

Published in 2015 by **Windmill Books**, An Imprint of Rosen Publishing
29 East 21st Street, New York, NY 10010

Adaptations to North American edition © 2015 Windmill Books
An Imprint of Rosen Publishing

Editor for Alix Wood Books: Eloise Macgregor
Designer: Alix Wood

Photo Credits: Cover, 1, 14, 20-21 © nga/Mr and Mrs Paul Mellon; 3, 4 bottom, 5, 16, 23
top © Shutterstock; 7, 13 © Ny Glyptotek; 9 © Smith College Museum of Art; 10 top © nga/
Chester Dale Collection; 4 top, 8, 15 top and bottom, 16 top © public domain; 10 © DXR; 11
© Metropolitan Museum of New York; 17 © Van Gogh Museum; 18 © Pushkin Mueum; 19
© Galleria Nazionale d'Arte Moderna; 22 © Artothek; 23 © nga/Rosenwald Collection; 25
top, 27 © Musée d'Orsay; 25 bottom © Igor Golovniov/Shutterstock; 28 © Trevor Coote;
29 © Ateneum

Library of Congress Cataloging-in-Publication Data

Wood, Alix.
 Paul Gauguin / Alix Wood.
     pages cm. — (Artists through the ages)
 Includes bibliographical references.
 Includes index.
ISBN 978-1-4777-5406-1 (pbk.)
ISBN 978-1-4777-5407-8 (6 pack)
ISBN 978-1-4777-5405-4 (library binding)
1. Gauguin, Paul, 1848-1903—Juvenile literature. 2. Artists—France—Biography—
Juvenile literature. I. Title.
 N6853.G34W66 2015
 759.4—dc23
 [B]

                              2014028088

Manufactured in the United States of America

CPSIA Compliance Information: Batch #CW15WM: For Further Information contact Windmill Books, New York, New York at 1-866-478-0556

Contents

Who Was Gauguin? 4

Family Man.................................6

Mixing with Artists......................8

Gauguin's Sculpture 10

Money Troubles 12

Leaving Family Behind...................14

Gauguin and Van Gogh..................16

The Night Café.........................18

Brittany...................................20

Gauguin in Tahiti 22

Women on the Beach 24

A Visit to France.........................26

Gauguin's Last Days......................28

Glossary...................................30

Websites..................................31

Read More and Index....................32

Who Was Gauguin?

Paul Gauguin was a **Postimpressionist** painter. He was born in Paris, France. His family moved to Peru in South America when he was very young. His father died on the long sea journey. Paul, his sister Marie, and his mother lived with an uncle in Lima, Peru for three years, until the family moved to Orléans, France.

Paul Gauguin

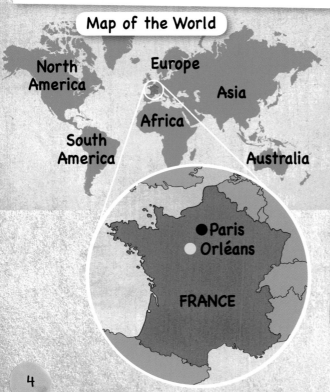

Map of the World

North America
Europe
Asia
Africa
South America
Australia

● Paris
○ Orléans

FRANCE

A view of the cathedral and river Loire at Orléans.

After a few years at local schools, Gauguin was sent to a Catholic boarding school. His mother moved back to Paris, and Gauguin visited her there in the holidays. After enrolling at a navy school, Gauguin joined the merchant navy at age 17, and then the French navy. For years he traveled the world, from South America to the Far East. He even sailed around the North Pole.

Gauguin's Mother and Peru

Gauguin's grandmother was half Peruvian. When in Lima, Gauguin's mother wore the local women's traditional costume, a veil that covered one eye. This costume would have seemed **exotic** in France at the time, but was normal in Peru. Gauguin's mother collected Peruvian pottery, and the images on the pottery influenced Gauguin's art.

A typical Peruvian pot, with bold, flat colors and black outlines.

Family Man

Gauguin's mother died while he was away on a ship. Her wealthy boyfriend, Gustave Arosa, got Gauguin a job working as a **stockbroker**. For the next 11 years Gauguin was a successful businessman. He married a Danish woman, Mette-Sophie. They had five children, Emil, Aline, Clovis, Jean René, and Paul. Gauguin painted in his spare time. He visited galleries in Paris and made friends with other artists. Gauguin earned enough money to start collecting art. He bought pictures by other artists such as Camille Pissarro and Paul Cézanne.

The Family of the Painter in the Garden, rue Carcel, 1881

Mixing with Artists

Gauguin became friends with the artist Camille Pissarro. He visited him on Sundays to paint in Pissarro's garden. Pissarro was older than Gauguin, and Gauguin admired him and his work. Pissarro was like a father figure to many Postimpressionist artists at the time, including Edgar Degas, Georges Seurat, Paul Cézanne, and Vincent van Gogh.

Pissarro introduced Gauguin to other artists such as Paul Cézanne, and they would spend summer holidays painting together. Pissarro encouraged Gauguin to **exhibit** paintings at Impressionist exhibitions.

Camille Pissarro

Gauguin's early paintings were quite different from his later work. He used more natural colors instead of the flat, bright colors he became known for later. He was very influenced by Pissarro's work at this time.

Masterclass

While still working as a stockbroker, Gauguin bought several paintings by Pissarro and Cézanne. He studied the brushstrokes and tried the styles for himself.

The Market Gardens of Vaugirard, Paul Gauguin, 1879

Gauguin's Sculpture

Gauguin changed jobs to work in a bank. The more regular business hours meant that he had more time for his art. Gauguin became interested in carving and **woodcuts**. Inspired by the **clogs** worn by country people, he carved his own and would wear them, even around the streets of fashionable Paris!

A pair of Gauguin's clogs

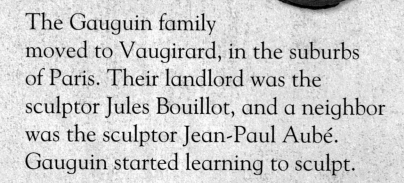

The Gauguin family moved to Vaugirard, in the suburbs of Paris. Their landlord was the sculptor Jules Bouillot, and a neighbor was the sculptor Jean-Paul Aubé. Gauguin started learning to sculpt.

The church of Saint-Lambert, Vaugirard

Gauguin's first piece of art that he exhibited was a sculpture, not a painting. Gauguin was invited by Pissarro and Degas to exhibit at the fourth **Impressionist** exhibition in Paris. He entered this sculpture of his son, Emil.

Late Entry

Gauguin was late entering his sculpture for the exhibition, so it was never put in the catalog. We know it was exhibited because people wrote about having seen it there.

Emil Gauguin. Gauguin sculpted this around 1877.

Money Troubles

In 1882 the French **stock market** crashed.
Gauguin lost his job at the bank as a result.
To support his family he began to paint full-time.
He also earned money selling life insurance, and
working as an agent for a sail-cloth company.

The family moved but Gauguin and his wife argued.
Mette and the children went to Copenhagen in
Denmark and Mette found a job teaching French.
She encouraged Gauguin to
move there too. Gauguin
wasn't happy in Denmark.
He didn't speak Danish.
His job selling tarpaulin
depressed him. He spent
his spare time painting.
He held an art exhibition
in Copenhagen, but it
closed after only five days!

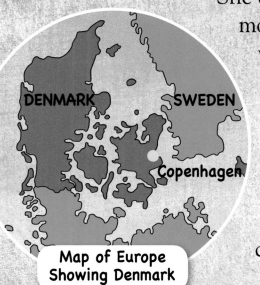

Map of Europe
Showing Denmark

The Queen's Mill, Østervold, 1885. Gauguin painted this while he was in Denmark.

Leaving Family Behind

While they were in Denmark the family stayed with
Mette's parents, the Gads. It was not a happy time for
Gauguin. After six months in Denmark, he returned
to Paris with his son Clovis, now 6 years old, and left
Mette with the other four children in Copenhagen.

Gauguin's *Still Life with Peonies*, 1884. The
inscription says in French "To Mr. Théodore Gad,
his friend." Théodore Gad was Mette's father.

Gauguin returned to Paris. He earned a living pasting posters on walls. He and Clovis lived in poverty until Gauguin's sister Marie helped out and paid for her nephew to go to boarding school. Gauguin then spent time painting and exhibited at the Eighth Impressionist Exhibition.

A typical French poster. This one advertises the Paris Exhibition of 1889.

The Feud with Seurat

Georges Seurat

At the same Impressionist exhibition a young painter, Georges Seurat, exhibited a painting called *A Sunday Afternoon on the Island of La Grande Jatte*. People loved the painting and this may have made Gauguin jealous. Another painter, Paul Signac, let Gauguin use his **studio** one day. Unaware of this, Seurat was already painting there and refused to let Gauguin in! From then on Gauguin disliked Seurat.

Gauguin and Van Gogh

Gauguin became friends with the artist Vincent van Gogh and his art dealer brother Theo. Gauguin agreed to visit Vincent in Arles where Vincent had dreams of setting up an artist's colony. They lived together in Vincent's "Yellow House."

Vincent van Gogh

Van Gogh liked to paint sunflowers. This is one of his paintings.

Theo paid the rent, and Vincent worked hard to make a comfortable space for the two to paint. Van Gogh admired Gauguin. The pair lived together for two months. They visited galleries, and Gauguin painted Vincent's portrait. Theo sold a number of Gauguin's works at an exhibition in Paris.

Van Gogh Painting Sunflowers, 1888. Gauguin did
this painting of his friend during his time in Arles.

At first the arrangement suited both artists.
After a while, however, they started to argue,
mainly about art. Both men were quite difficult
characters. Gauguin was considered **arrogant**
and Van Gogh was moody.

The Night Café

Arles café owner Madame Ginoux sat for Van Gogh and Gauguin in their shared studio. Gauguin created the painting below, and later Van Gogh painted his own portrait based on Gauguin's painting. Both artists also painted Monsieur Ginoux.

Le Café de Nuit, Paul Gauguin, 1888

Van Gogh and Gauguin painted similar subjects in similar styles. They painted the same landscapes and people in the village. Gauguin bought a bale of **jute** material, which both artists used for their **canvases**. The material was coarse and they both had to use heavier brushstrokes and thicker paint.

L'Arlésienne, Van Gogh, 1890

The Argument and the Ear

One evening Vincent and Gauguin had an argument. Gauguin claimed Vincent threatened him with a knife. It is believed that later that evening Vincent went home and cut off a section of his left ear. He then wrapped the ear in cloth and gave it as a present to a woman he knew. The police were called and Vincent was taken to the hospital. Some people believe that Gauguin cut Van Gogh's ear in the argument, and Van Gogh made up the story to protect his friend.

Brittany

Gauguin visited Le Pouldu and Pont Aven in Brittany, France and painted with the Dutch artist Jacob Meyer de Haan, who paid their rent and bought their food.

Gauguin was followed there by the young artist Paul Sérusier who admired him. Gauguin helped Sérusier. He advised him to stop using Pissarro's style of painting. Gauguin now preferred strong outlines and simple bold colors like in his painting on the right.

Eventually Meyer de Haan's family stopped sending them money, and Gauguin was forced to return to Paris.

Landscape at Le Pouldu, 1890

Gauguin in Tahiti

In 1891 Gauguin held a public sale of his work to raise money to pay for a sea voyage. Gauguin wanted to live and paint in Tahiti, a group of small islands in the South Pacific Ocean. Gauguin dreamed of a **tropical paradise**.

Two Woman from Tahiti, 1899

Tahiti

Pacific
Ocean

Tahiti

**Map Showing the
Pacific Ocean and Tahiti**

He arrived in Pape'ete, Tahiti ill with **bronchitis**. It was not the perfect life he had hoped for. Imported art supplies were very expensive. The local people didn't accept him. Gauguin headed away from the town and to a shack in a village.

Woodcuts

Gauguin created a magazine for French settlers called *Le Sourire* which means "the smile." He carved woodcuts to print the pages.

Women on the Beach

Gauguin is probably most well-known for his paintings from the islands of Tahiti. Gauguin enjoyed looking at and painting the scenery and the people.

Primitivism

Gauguin was one of the leading artists in a movement called "Primitivism." There was a fascination at the time for people from less-developed countries. The people were thought to be more genuine and **spiritual** than the "artificial" Europeans and Americans.

The two women in the painting *Tahitian Women on the Beach* look quite miserable and uneasy. It's not the sort of painting you would expect. The two women are sitting close together but are not looking at each other. Often in Gauguin's Tahitian paintings the subjects have their backs turned to the painter. He wanted to show the local people's mysterious natures.

Tahitian Women on the Beach, 1891

Gauguin painted several versions of the same painting. This stamp shows another version. Can you see the differences?

A Visit to France

There were no art collectors in Tahiti and Gauguin became forgotten in the art world in Paris. To earn some money Gauguin sent eight of his Tahitian paintings to Mette in Copenhagen. She got them into an exhibition. The show was a success, but Gauguin wanted to be a success in Paris.

Gauguin used the last of his money and sailed back to France. His health was not good. He held a solo exhibition but the Paris art world did not know what to make of his Tahiti paintings. He only sold 11 of the 44 he exhibited. Disappointed, Gauguin moved back to Pont Aven.

Pont Aven

When Gauguin returned to France he went to the artists commune he had helped form in Pont Aven, ten years before. The artists had developed a style called "Synthetism." It was quite different from Impressionism, with no shading and no unnecessary detail.

Watermill in Pont-Aven, 1894

That summer Gauguin was badly beaten in a
fight with a group of sailors. While recovering in
the hospital, his new partner, Anna the Javanese,
went to his Paris studio and stole everything of
value there. Gauguin held another sale of his art to
finance his return to Tahiti. Not many people went,
but he sold a few paintings, mainly to friends.

Gauguin's Last Days

Gauguin sailed back to Pape'ete. He began building a house with a large studio, but became ill. Gauguin left Tahiti and moved to the French Marquesas islands. The Marquesans were more welcoming than the Tahitians had been. Gauguin was more comfortable and happier there, but he was in poor health and died at age 55 on the island of Hiva Oa.

Gauguin's paintings were mostly only appreciated after his death. Today Gauguin is recognized as one of the fathers of modern art. His use of patterns and remarkable color combinations inspired other artists. He also played an important part in bringing back the art of woodcutting.

Gauguin's grave on Hiva Oa

Landscape on La Dominique, 1903
was one of Gauguin's last paintings.

Glossary

arrogant (AHR-uh-gant)
Overly proud of oneself or one's own opinions.

bronchitis (bron-KY-tis)
An illness of the lungs.

canvases (KAN-vuh-sehz)
Pieces of cloth used as a surface for painting.

clogs (KLOGS)
A shoe with a thick usually wooden sole.

exhibit (ehk-ZIH-biht)
Put something such as a painting on show.

exotic (ehk-ZAH-tik)
Very different or unusual, often introduced from another country.

Impressionist (im-PREH-shuh-nist)
An artist who concentrates on the impression of a scene using unmixed primary colors and small brushstrokes to simulate light.

jute (JOOT)
A fiber used chiefly for making sacks and twine.

Postimpressionist
(POHST-im-PREH-shuh-nist)
An artist who reacted
against the naturalism of
the Impressionists.

spiritual (SPEER-ih-choo-ul)
Sacred or religious.

stockbroker
(STOK BROH-kur)
A person who buys and
sell stocks.

stock market
(STOK MAR-ket)
A place where people buy
and sell stocks.

studio (STOO-dee-oh)
The working place of
an artist.

tropical paradise
(TRAH-pih-kihl
PEHR-uh-dys)
A place in the tropics where
everything is as you would
like it to be.

woodcut
(WOOD-kut)
A printing surface having
a raised design carved from
a block of wood.

Websites

For web resources related to the
subject of this book, go to:
www.windmillbooks.com/weblinks
and select this book's title.

Read More

Kerellis, Helene. *The Color of the Night: A Children's Book Inspired by Paul Gauguin*. New York, NY: Prestel, 2012.

Merberg, Julie. *On An Island With Gauguin*. San Francisco: Chronicle Books, 2007.

Spence, David. *Gauguin*. *TickTock Essential Artists*. London: TickTock, 2008.

Index

A

Arlésienne, La 19
Arosa, Gustave 6
Aubé, Jean-Paul 10

B

Bouilliot, Jules 10

C

Café de Nuit, Le 18
Cézanne, Paul 6, 8, 9

D

Degas, Edgar 8, 11

F

Family of the Painter in the Garden, rue Carcel, The 7

G

Gauguin, Emil 11
Gauguin, Mette-Sophie 6, 12, 14, 26

L

Landscape on La Dominique 29

M

Market Gardens of Vaugirard, The 9
Meyer de Haan, Jacob 20

P

Pissarro, Camille 6, 8, 9, 11, 20

Q

Queen's Mill, Østervold, The 13

S

Seurat, Georges 8, 15
Still Life with Peonies 14

T

Tahitian Women on the Beach 25
Two Women from Tahiti 22

V

Van Gogh Painting Sunflowers 17
Van Gogh, Theo 16
Van Gogh, Vincent 8, 16, 17, 18, 19

W

Watermill in Pont-Aven 27